Whispers of the blue ghost

Pratikshya Panda

BookLeaf
Publishing

India | USA | UK

Presentation by *BookLeaf Publishing*

Web: www.bookleafpub.com

E-mail: info@bookleafpub.com

ISBN: 9789363312807

First edition 2024

To bapa and maa

Tall Poppy Dreams

Black pebbles on grey beaches
crawling away from the foamy waves.
The sea is so grey like a thousand dreams died in
it.
We are always lost in it
So we never have the time to find ourselves.
From the moon we watch
As all our screams get lost in Saturn's mouth
What is it that we want?
What is it that souls are made of?
What is it that dying babies dream of?
What is it that tall poppies cry about?
The same thing, I guess.

Ghost of the Burning River

The river is loud.
The river is loud, and my eyes are burning.
And as I look at the sky, I can see flecks of
hollowness falling,
It piles up on the floor and creeps under my feet,
and I feel voids forming inside me.
Orange sunshine dancing on the haze that flies
away from my skin,
Swirling and swirling until it gets scattered in
the wind.
Never to be seen again,
Never to be felt again.

I can remember a time,
Perhaps a million storms ago—when the river
wasn't loud.

Instead, it made music.
It made music as the same orange sunshine
danced on its waves.
And my not-so-developed brain thought that the
river was burning.
The river was burning, and still, it was cold and
perfect and beautiful.
And I used to look at the sky and could see
flecks of bliss falling.
falling and falling and making layers on my
skin.

Maybe the sun won't shed flecks of happiness
anymore.
Maybe I will count my time in seasons and
storms forever.
Maybe I will come here again and again and
again, and I will never hear music anymore.
And the river will be obnoxiously devastatingly
loud.
And it will never burn quite so beautifully again,
But it will be fine.
As long as I get to see the same sunlight and
close my eyes and can almost feel like I don't
have any voids,
And the red I always see in my dreams is the
ghost of the burning river.

The Blue Ghost

She used to say the sky is solid.
And I wondered why doesn't it ever fall apart.
She would say the sky doesn't crumble.
It drips.
Now, when I close my eyes, I dream blue.
When I open my eyes, I see blue.
The blue ghost that hovers above me is funny.
It doesn't let me go.
It once dipped a paintbrush in its eyes and
painted the walls blue.
I've sewn back fallen petals to dead stems
hoping it would become what it was again.
Red and yellow—like flame.
The blue ghost laughs.
And it feels like taking a bite out of the ice.

I thought I had not turned blue yet
and opened myself.
But the bright red drops that fell on my floor
turned stale and blue.
I would do it again and again and see
It's not bright red anymore.
I once said, "The people with the sun behind
their eyes like it—the blue sky,
the cerulean ocean,
they don't cry when corpses of stars turn blue
and fall on their face."
The blue ghost asked,
"Do you?"
Taking a bite out of the ice again.
When I lay down with the blue ghost by my
side,
I feel like smoke.
Parts of me fly away through the window,
and I think they will get lost in the sky.
But they come back.
And now I know why.
The sky is solid.
It never lets you escape.
I'm sure it doesn't crumble or drip.
It vomits the blue corpses of stars and all its
grief
that stay by my side,
the blue ghost.

Corpses of Butterflies

The morning is warm.
Where the crimson spills from the sky and
blends in the dew.
Blood drops on the grass.
It reminds me of you, my love.
You—with your love of photography—and dead
butterflies that swim in the scarlet ocean
You smile and light flickers in the sky
One by one by one
Maybe I should lie down here on the grass,
taking in the silence of the comatose morning
Maybe you'll come and pick me up
and pin my tattered wings down on one of your
fancy wooden frames
I think I'll be able to look you in the eyes then
and hate you
while my heart still beats.

Drunk Night/Dead Dreams

The night is drunk
and tired after years and years of nocturnal rain
where it bleeds and bleeds and the world is
asleep.
It asks,
"Tell me, what kind of hope hoarder are you?
Writing your own myths
leaving kiss marks on every brittle bone
and smiling as if the sun sits in your mouth."
And no one answers
'cause the hope hoarders are asleep
Those who are awake
bleed dead dreams with the night.

Maths

A bed,
A nighttime story,
$34\times15=510$,
Chapped lips on my forehead.
That's what I think of when I close my eyes
In this city where my blood has turned into
poison
That's what I think of when I lay on the damp
grass after heavy rain
and sultry sunlight falls on my face.
My bed is unmade for days
And my body is stained with ridge marks of lips
that sting like acid
And I still close my eyes and say
$17\times24=408$

and pretend the princess will leave the kingdom
behind anytime soon
with a warm hand on her forehead, telling her to
sleep.

Dandelions

Maybe in another life
We were grieving dandelion—
fluffs from the same flower
But when summer came, we drifted apart
Far, far, far.
Maybe you bloomed at a children's park
And I at a riverside.
Maybe your leaves were just a little crooked at
the edge, like mine
And maybe my flower was the same shade of
yellow as yours.
And maybe we sometimes forget that

as we run across the field stepping over all those
flowers in grief.
Aren't we all just the same?

To you

One day, I walked down the fish market
saw an old friend, and we laughed and talked.
His grin split his face into two when he told me
he wished I were dead.
The other day, I was staring at the walls of the
new flat I moved into.
The landlady put her arm around me and smiled
saying how she'll never allow me to live here.
My friends, lovers, the whole city
dreams I shouldn't exist.
I stare at the mirror in the college washroom and
repeat what they say
I stare at the mirror in my room and scream.

Footsteps

Footsteps that sound like the clicking of laptop
keys
Without rhythm
That is what I'm familiar with.
Daisies hide under sunlight
When the day arrives with its shadowy curtain
and they have nowhere to go at night
As moonlight curls around their neck and
tightens
And what is it that I do?
When I hide from the moonlight, run away from
the sun.
But the moonlight isn't chasing me, is it?
The sun couldn't care less
If I drink my coffee at eight

or Lurata at nine
Who am I running to?
Who am I running from?
All these questions are like
a person who doesn't know anything about piano
playing it
And it rings in my ear
But I am familiar with footsteps that sound like
the clicking of laptop keys
Mine.

Small talks

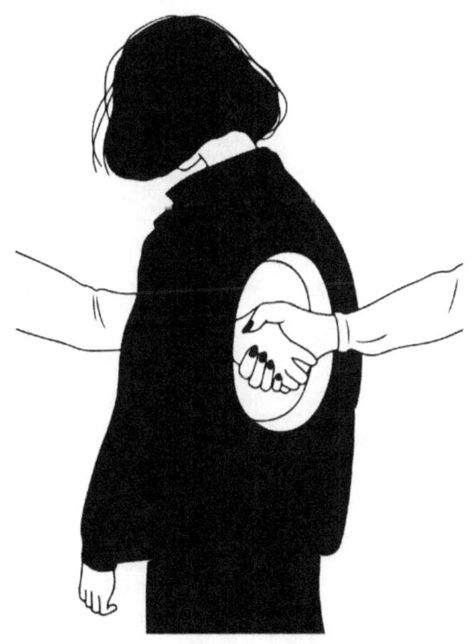

"Yes, the weather is nice today.
Do you remember when we did that—
We were so naive
We were so stupid."
That's all I've got to say.
Once upon a time, butterflies lived forever.
Funny little monsters they were,
Fluttering around with their glittery veins
And our high tide heartbeats never tamed.
At that moment, I wished to live forever.
And still, all I can talk about now is
Yes, of course, the weather is so nice today.

And you'll go back to the world you've built
And I to mine.
I wonder if—in yours—butterflies still live
forever—
Because mine are dying creatures
with ash-filled veins.

3:15

The roses that spilled mercury
all over the floor died today
I remember that night you wore moon
like a scared little child hiding under a blanket
And I talked like my throat was filled with glass
bubbles of giggles
That burst out at every few words
And you drank everything
The mercury, the words, the giggles, the blood
that spilled from my throat.
How can I bury the rose
And not think about you
melting everywhere,

On the floor, in the sky, on my lips.
We are buried in that night
tucked in our moon blanket
We shall never be that alive again.

Mother

In the creaks of my satin sheets
I hide my tears, guilt, and blunt knives
that stick out when it's dark.
Mother,
only if you knew what I think
The eyes that open their lid in the dark,
Zig zag, left to the right, right to the left like a
haunted pendulum,
The pool of bone marrow under my skin
There is no time for sweetness.
There is no space for God.
Mother,
I still remember
The red polka dots of your saree
that you veiled on my face whenever I got
scared of the sun.
Mother,
Only if you knew I'm still scared.

Misery has a colour

Misery has a colour.
Just like home, freedom and
the touch that lingers on one's skin like a big
crawling snake.
How does it look?
The sky is always grey.
The air drips grey onto the earth as it weeps.
And my blood is hot, rotten green poison.
I am hollow, and the poison runs on my skin,
It never burns.
It never stops aching like it does.

Death, murder, suicide

It came like sudden hiccups
or winter rain
things you don't expect,
things you can't plan for.
I still think about those 12 PM dreams
that suicided just like that
and I was left again
with debris of what could've been
so I wear white again
to mourn the loss of stars and the moon
The thing that shines in the sky is nothing but
a ghost of a long, dead dream.
Was it death or murder or suicide
I'll never know
I never got a chance to ask the dreams
If they dream of being alive.

Red

I know nothing
of the way my mother's hands branch into
thousands
or the way my father disappear in the ocean of
our living room
I think she swallowed a God when she was little
and he a galaxy
How else will I explain
How they shielded me from the ghosts with a
piece of warmth on my face
so I tried to swallow a God too
But I threw up
My body a mess on the floor, throat cracked.

Five-year-old me developed a sandpaper tongue
that peels my mouth off whenever I speak
or so I thought
till the day when I screamed
and threw up red red things everywhere
my tongue was flesh again
My mother called the red a God, or love
that was always inside me.

Fame

From up above the sky so high
You stare at the black and the black stares back
The language of moon is so ancient.
Yet you never understood
Why it sings, what it laments.
You stare at the ground and they stare back,
Empty blackhole eyes
Devouring every little thing you throw at them.
Lonely little thing lost in the crowd,
Is it worth it?
Fame's cold embrace

Moondust

Have you ever held
a skin that stretches forever
Wrinkled and crumpled from laughing too much.
I can see the pink moondust
That fell on my bed every day
Seeping into my skin, making me an addict
Worse than cocaine heads stumbling face-first
into drains.
I dream of holding that heart again

It beats travelling along its walls
Alive, alive, alive.
And I realised I could never hand my beating
heart to someone
like I held hers once.
Looking at the fuzzy silhouettes of neon
blinking stars on my ceiling,
Fever seeps deep into my skin
Was the tip of my hair this dry
When I sat on those stairs
And saw the moondust for the first time.
It's raining moondust again
And my heart is on my feet.

Hungry things

Do you think the sun feels it too?
Belly aches and dry throats after hours of
laughing.
The world is set on flames
And the growing pain in my heart is settling
on the road to home, at the corner of my room,
Along with a thousand other things.
Maybe the moon feels it too
itch of the mouth after decades of hunger
It can't swallow the earth
It can't swallow the sky
It swallows the orange sunshine and pulls waves
And grows red, red, red.
Making poets die of heartaches
The world is too big for our palms
And we are too small for our dreams
The earth is spinning too fast
Hurling us into the sky
Body on Mars, A shoe on a star, and soul forever
in purgatory
Can we touch the raindrop on the ground
And feel what it felt at the high of the sky

What about the drop at the bottom of the ocean
That does not know it is capable of creating
rainbows?

Midnight ghost

Midnight creeps onto my bed at 7 AM
There's a ghost in my house
Spilling bottles of sleep
and knitting nightmares out of the moonlight
That peeps into my bedroom through the small
hole in my window
It asks all sorts of questions
I tell him I am away
He tells me he is away
Yet when I talk, my lips open
but the voice is the ghost's

What kills a poet

The chair in my room is crumbling
Its wooden legs broken at the weight of fat
dreams
Every corner is lost somewhere
Following a light that comes from nowhere
That goes nowhere
I have left my limbs in room no. 211
of that hostel
And my organs splattered on that road to school
that stretched forever
like the loose rubber-band

that is lost everywhere
I just have a heart left
And a pair of eyes
that refuse to be thrown away
I have perched those eyes on the broken chair
And it is breaking still
What kills a poet?
Forty grams of grief?
The extinction of moon?
A heart attack?
Bullets?
Spilling guts on paper?
Fat Dreams.

Paper boat

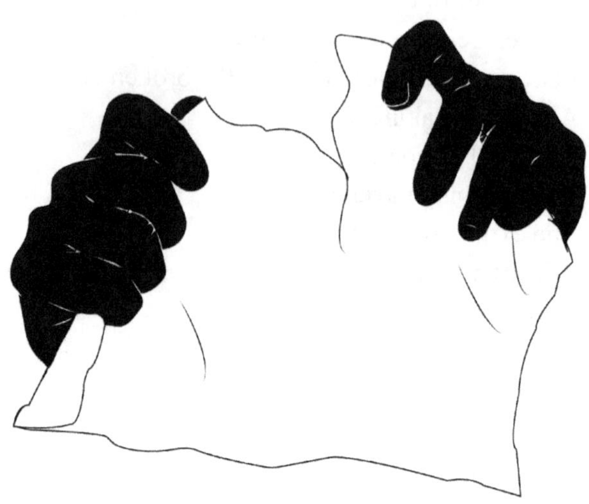

I am a paper boat.
sailing through seas
With my body crumpled and leaking.
I wasn't made to last
I wasn't made to thrive
In a world where whispers can drown a scream.